W9-DFD-973

REAL WORLD ECONOMICS™

How
Globalization
Works

Laura La Bella

ROSEN
PUBLISHING®

New York

For my brother, Paul

Published in 2010 by The Rosen Publishing Group, Inc.
29 East 21st Street, New York, NY 10010

Library of Congress Cataloging-in-Publication Data

La Bella, Laura.
How globalization works / Laura La Bella.—1st ed.
   p. cm.—(Real world economics)
Includes bibliographical references and index.
ISBN-13: 978-1-4358-5323-2 (library binding)
1. Globalization. I. Title.
JZ1318.L334 2009
303.48'2—dc22

2008049579

Manufactured in Malaysia

On the cover: A McDonald's employee delivers a drive-through order at this fast food franchise in Beijing, China. The first McDonald's opened in mainland China in 1990, and now more than 760 McDonald's restaurants employing 50,000 people are in operation in that country.

Contents

INTRODUCTION

When you visit your local supermarket, you purchase foods from a number of different countries. The grapes you buy might be from Chile. Or, the tomatoes you picked up might have been grown in Mexico.

If you encounter a problem with your computer, you might call a help desk. The person you are talking to might actually live and work in India.

Go to the mall and look at the tags on the clothes that you like to buy. Many will say that the items were made in China, Indonesia, or El Salvador.

This is globalization.

Take a look at McDonald's, the largest fast-food restaurant chain in the world, as an example of how a company might approach globalization. McDonald's operates more than 31,000 restaurants in at least 107 countries around the world. Each day, it serves more than 58 million people. But what is unique about McDonald's is that, throughout the world, its menus

reflect the cultures of the countries in which it has restaurants. Here in the United States, stop into any McDonald's and the most popular menu items might be the Big Mac, Chicken McNuggets, and the chain's famous french fries.

In India, however, most people do not eat beef due to their religious beliefs, which include honoring cows as sacred animals. You won't find hamburgers on the menu at a McDonald's there. Instead, the menu items at McDonald's restaurants in India are all vegetarian. The most popular item is the Veggie Burger, which is a hamburger-like sandwich that's made from potatoes, peas, and carrots, and is flavored with Indian spices. Even the soft-serve ice cream at an Indian McDonald's has a special recipe that does not use eggs, which is another food item that Hindus in India do not eat.

The same consideration for local tastes and customs is extended to McDonald's restaurants in other countries around the world. In Japan, a Teriyaki McBurger replaces the Big Mac.

Indian employees work at a call center in the city of Bangalore. India's call centers provide inexpensive English-speaking workers and high-speed telecommunication technology that offer customer service to companies around the world.

In Norway, customers can order the McLaks, which is a salmon burger. McDonald's is an example of an American company growing beyond its borders while making sure that local customs are reflected in its menus. This, too, is globalization.

You can't escape globalization. "Globalization"—or "globalism," as it is also often called—is a term that became popular in the 1980s. It describes the increased international movement of people, knowledge, ideas, products, and money. All of this movement has increased the interconnectedness among the world's populations. It has also made possible the merging of economic, political, social, and cultural identities.

Globalization occurs when companies, products, and services spread to other countries. This starts influencing the cultures and people in those countries. The process of globalization begins when there is a demand for a product that a particular country doesn't have or cannot produce. For example, Americans need gasoline to fuel their cars. Gasoline is produced from oil. But in the United States, there is not enough oil available to meet the demand. Therefore, the United States has to buy oil from other countries in order to create gasoline so that Americans can power their cars and trucks.

While it is a powerful economic force, globalization can be both good and bad. Its effect on the world has been both positive and negative. Globalization can create business opportunities for growing companies. This results in new jobs. It gives people access to products and services that they might not otherwise have in their own countries. And it can aid in a new understanding of cultures, languages, and customs that are different from our own. But globalization has a downside, too. It can cause a loss of native (original or home-gown) culture and heritage as people adapt to outside, foreign influences. It can cause job loss as local businesses build companies in other countries where it costs less to pay workers. Globalization can help some countries grow and expand their workforce, even if it costs other countries much-needed jobs. It can also harm the environment.

Globalization is not a new concept. In fact, for thousands of years, countries have bought products from and sold goods to other countries. In the 1800s, the East India Company, which was established in Great Britain, brought cotton, silk, dye, and tea to America's shores for sale. Russia was a major supplier of fur pelts to western Europe and parts of Asia. The pace, scope, and scale of globalization have accelerated dramatically since World War II, especially in the last twenty-five years. Today, there are countless examples of products that are produced in other countries and sold globally. Sometimes, the company that makes the product is based in a different country from that in which the product is actually made. And that product may be sold in a third country or even worldwide.

Globalization has an impact on technology, health, culture, immigration, the development of poor nations, the environment, and the production of energy to power our homes and businesses.

CHAPTER ONE

Types of Globalization

There are different types of globalization. Examining and understanding each of them allows us to see how globalization works in many ways. It also lets us see how nations and their cultures affect one another.

Economic Globalization

When we use the words "economic globalization," we are really talking about how money travels around the world. Each country has its own businesses, and these businesses often sell their products outside of their own country. When people from many countries around the world are able to buy products that are made and sold by foreign companies— and even work for these companies in some cases—a connection is forged among many different nations. The products we buy and the jobs we have that come from foreign businesses connect us to other countries, their culture, and their peoples.

Economic globalization has been occurring for several thousand years, but it has begun to occur at an increased rate over the last twenty to thirty years. This recent boom has seen the economies of more developed nations partnering with the economies of less developed countries.

For example, Toyota Motor Company is a Japanese carmaker that has manufacturing and assembly factories in more than twenty-five countries, including the United States, Mexico, France, Brazil, Turkey, and Thailand. These factories provide jobs and a paycheck to the workers in these nations. The workers, in turn, spend that money to buy products from not only their own countries but from countries around the world as well. For many companies that make large products like cars, production might occur in more than one country. Cars are often produced in multiple countries by different teams of workers. A new car may be designed in one country, its parts could be manufactured in a second country, and the assembly of those parts might occur in a third country. The breakdown or separating out of jobs is called a division of labor. Today, this division can take place in different countries.

Sometimes, companies in one country produce more goods and services than can be used by its own population. In other words, there aren't enough people in the country to use all of what is made there. The Ivory Coast, located in Africa, is one of the largest producers of cocoa. It sells what it cannot use to other countries that need it. Countries will often pay for goods and services that they either cannot make themselves or are of a higher quality than what they can manufacture.

Other times, countries cannot produce enough of a product that is in great need, so they buy products from other countries.

Auto workers in Alabama assemble cars at a Hyundai plant. Hyundai, a Korean car company, has manufacturing plants and research and development centers in Korea, the United States, China, Pakistan, India, Turkey, and Japan, and throughout Europe.

This is the case with the earlier example of oil. The United States uses more than 25 percent of the world's oil, but it produces only 3 percent of the world's oil supply. To keep cars running and homes heated, the United States must purchase oil from other countries in order to fill the demand.

Economic globalization is one of the few types of globalization that can be measured. We can look at four different categories to see if economic globalization has increased or decreased around the world. These four categories are:

- Goods and services, which are measured in terms of the number of products that are exported (sold and

The United States uses more than 25 percent of the world's oil supply. This oil tanker, anchored off the coast of Southern California, delivers oil to America from other countries.

sent to other countries from the United States) or imported (sold and sent to the United States from other countries)

- Migration, or movement of people, which allows us to watch how many people come into a country to find work or how many are forced to leave to find work outside that country

- Capital, or money, which helps gauge how much each nation makes as a result of products and people flowing back and forth

- Technology, which tells us how inventions and innovations in communication, computers, and manufacturing influence globalization

Political Globalization

Political globalization is how governments from different countries get along with one another. The United States has countries that it is very friendly with (such as England, France, Japan, and Canada) and other countries that it is not so friendly with (Iran, North Korea, Cuba, and Syria, for example).

Technology, such as the Internet, cell phones, jet planes, and satellite television, has connected people in different countries, whether they be friend or foe. This connectivity has increased our awareness of one another because we can see and talk to each other instantly. This allows us to see what other countries are doing and encourages our governments to develop relationships with one other, even if there are disagreements, suspicion, or bad feelings. Those relationships can be helpful when we form partnerships to help defend ourselves against common enemies, to deliver help following a natural disaster (such as a hurricane or earthquake), and to exchange scientific information like cures for diseases.

Thanks in large part to the emissions of manufacturers worldwide, pollution enters the atmosphere and can harm the environment. Acid rain has damaged this forest on Mount Mitchell in North Carolina.

Ecological Globalization

Ecological globalization refers to the influence people and companies have on the world's ecosystems. An ecosystem con-

sists of all the plants, animals, and microorganisms that work together in the environment of a specific area. A rain forest is an example of an ecosystem. Ecosystems are constantly changing. The movement of air over the surface of the earth, the flow of water in rivers, and the migration of animals and people across a landscape all cause changes in ecosystems.

For example, the West Coast of the United States is affected by the air pollution that is created in China and other Asian countries. Tiny airborne particles of pollution are drifting over the Pacific Ocean from coal-fired power plants, smelters, dust storms, and diesel trucks in Asia. This causes harm to the air and water quality and to the general environmental health of American cities on the West Coast, such as San Francisco.

A Global Act of Caring: Relief Aid During the Asian Tsunami

On December 26, 2004, an earthquake in the Indian Ocean caused a tsunami, a series of massive waves that can cause immense flooding and destruction. Particularly hard-hit were India, Indonesia, Sri Lanka, and Thailand. More than 225,000 people were killed, tens of thousands were injured, and 10 million found

Aid workers organize food, clothing, and medical supplies that were donated by relief organizations and foreign countries for the tsunami victims.

themselves homeless. The world's response to this tragedy is an example of political globalization. Governments and companies from around the world provided help to the countries affected by the natural disaster. More than fifty-five countries offered military help and monetary aid. In addition, millions of people donated money to help, and companies worldwide offered their support. Pharmaceutical (drug) companies like Pfizer, Johnson & Johnson, and Bristol-Myers Squibb provided medical supplies and drugs. Beverage companies, such as Iceland Spring Water, supplied fresh water. And humanitarian organizations—including the International Red Cross, Catholic Relief Services, Oxfam, the United Nations, and World Jewish Aid—donated medical supplies and services, sent volunteers, or raised money to help the tsunami victims rebuild their homes and communities.

To help keep the environment healthy on a global scale, people and companies worldwide must take into consideration the effects that their activities have on communities in countries outside of their own.

Cultural Globalization

Cultural globalization refers to the sharing of ideas and cultural products. The United States is the largest exporter of movies and, thus, is a large exporter of American culture. Other countries produce films, too. In fact, India produces more films a year than Hollywood does, and Japan and Hong Kong are leaders in movie production as well. However, many of these films are not seen outside of their home countries. Indian films are produced mostly for Indian audiences, and films from Japan and Hong Kong are shown outside of Asia in small "art house" movie theaters. Foreign films often have trouble getting distributed and shown in the United States, and they often don't come out on DVD.

Hollywood movies may showcase American ways of life, but the film industry is not uniquely American. Hollywood is known for finding the best actors, actresses, and directors from around the world and making them stars. *Pirates of the Caribbean* star Orlando Bloom is from England, *Chicago's* Catherine Zeta-Jones is from Wales, *Star Wars'* Ewan McGregor is from Scotland, and *X-Men's* Hugh Jackman is from Australia. Even some of Hollywood's top directors are from outside America. Ridley Scott, director of *Gladiator*, *Kingdom of Heaven*, and *Blade Runner*, is from England. Peter Jackson, the director of the three *Lord of the Rings* films, is from New Zealand. The *Harry Potter* movies, which have become the biggest film series in movie history, are based on books by an English author—J. K. Rowling—and feature a largely English cast. Some of Hollywood's biggest studios are also foreign-owned. Japan's Sony Company owns Columbia Pictures, and Vivendi Universal is French-owned.

A cultural phenomenon that has caught on in the United States is manga. *Manga* in Japanese basically means "comics," and it has become a large part of Japan's publishing industry. Manga stories include a broad range of subjects, from action-adventure, romance, and sports, to historical drama, comedy, science fiction, and horror. *Pokémon* is probably the most popular example of Japanese manga in the United States. The vast majority of manga sold in America is written, drawn, inked, and published in Japan. However, a small but growing American manga industry has sprung up in recent years.

Globalization of Communication

Globalization of communication is how the world's people talk to one another through more advanced technology. One hundred years ago, people communicated with each other by sending a letter or a telegram. Over the course of the last century, we have developed new ways to reach out to people instantaneously, even if they are in countries on the other side of the world. Today, cell phones, e-mail, text messaging, web-cams, and the Internet allow us to express our ideas instantly with others. Telecommunications companies like Verizon, Sprint, and AT&T all compete against each other to provide the fastest and easiest ways to communicate with other people via landline phone, cell phone, e-mail, and the Internet.

Apple's iPhone, which, in addition to cellular phone service, features Internet access, text messaging, a global positioning system, and other navigation aids, can connect its users to nearly anyone, anywhere. Here, a user views a metro, or subway, map of Paris, France.

These technologies allow for a greater amount of information to be exchanged back and forth between people and places that traditionally have not communicated with one another. As a result, there has been an increase in cross-cultural communication, understanding, and curiosity. Anyone with an Internet connection can access foreign news outlets—like the *Central Daily News* in North Korea, the *New Zealand Herald* in New Zealand, or the *People's Daily Newspaper* in China— just as easily as he or she can access CNN or *USA Today*.

CHAPTER TWO

The How's and Why's of Globalization

M cDonald's serves more people every day throughout the world than there are people living in the countries of Greece, Iceland, and Switzerland combined. The General Motors car company employs more people in its international manufacturing and assembly plants than the number of people who occupy most small nations. Every year, Domino's Pizza earns enough money from the sale of pizza and other fast-food items to support the economies of several nations, including Bolivia and Iceland. How does this occur? How do businesses grow so big and expand internationally? The answer is globalization.

Globalization occurs for many reasons. There have been advances in transportation and technology that make it much easier to produce goods and move them around the world quickly and relatively inexpensively. The creation and development of information and communications technology, particularly the Internet, allow people to raise their awareness

Federal Express cargo jets are lined up outside the company's world headquarters in Memphis, Tennessee. These planes, part of a fleet of more than 675 jets, will deliver packages and documents to destinations around the world, often overnight.

of different cultures and places. People are now much more knowledgeable about foreign foods and cultures, different languages, and international problems than they were in the past. It is now easier for people to communicate with others in faraway places, and even connect to one another through the Internet or satellite communications. Advances in communication technology help to spread globalization. Communication among people is now easier, faster, and cheaper (or even free in some cases) with the Internet and e-mail. The media, too, can now reach worldwide audiences, instantly broadcasting news and entertainment worldwide.

Cost-cutting is another important reason for globalization. Many well-known companies have a global presence and conduct business in countries around the world. They often open factories in other nations for a variety of economic reasons. Labor may be less expensive in other countries, which can save companies money. International trade also makes it easier to manufacture goods in the countries that consume them, cutting down on shipping costs.

Globalization is a complex issue. There are many people who are supportive of globalization. They believe it is a way to help poorer countries develop their economies and improve the lives of their citizens. But there are also those who are against globalization and think it ultimately hurts the workers and economies of both the home country and its foreign trading partners.

The Pro-Globalization Argument

Those who support globalization say that it has led to an increase in communication between peoples. It has had a positive impact on our environment. It has helped spread technology around the world. And it has aided in the movement of people who choose to live and work in other countries.

Supporters of globalization say that it can increase economic success and offer opportunities for developing nations, too. These opportunities can be an increase in the jobs available and higher pay for workers. Globalization can also lead to enhanced freedoms for the people living in developing countries. For example, workers might organize a union that will represent them in order to gain pay increases and better benefits, such as health care. Proponents also say that globalization can lead to the more efficient allocation (providing and spreading) of resources.

Globalization can result in competition between international companies. This keeps businesses sharp and forces them to develop new products and improve existing ones. Consumers benefit from this competition because it means that they have greater choices, a broader range of quality in the items offered, and, often, lower prices.

The spread of technology has been a positive outcome of globalization. Companies are establishing factories and offices in different countries, bringing with them new technologies that might not reach some underdeveloped countries otherwise.

Globalization also means the spread of people. Because globalization has increased the flow of information, improved communication, made transportation faster and cheaper, and increased the number of jobs available in some countries, it has caused workers to move or migrate to other countries.

In the city of New Delhi, India, thousands of cars and motorcycles hit the road every day, creating traffic jams and causing smog. Many residents of the city now suffer from itchy eyes, sore throats, and persistent coughs caused by car exhaust.

The migration of people is not new. For centuries, people have left their homes in search of better opportunities, both in and outside of their own countries. Globalization has just added a new dimension. As businesses expand to include operations in foreign countries, migration becomes a necessity for many.

Is Anything Really "Made in America" Anymore?

There was once a popular bumper sticker that appeared on the back of American-made cars that read, "Real Americans Buy American." But are products really made in America anymore?

American automobiles are a great example of American products that are not made entirely in the United States. Chevrolet, a popular U.S. car and truck company, builds many of its vehicles in Mexico with parts imported from other countries. The Ford Motor Company has plants all around the world. Its plant in Germany employs many workers who have emigrated from Turkey.

An American car designer created the Toyota Camry. Toyota, a Japanese automaker, owns a plant in Newport Beach, California, where the company has a design center. Its Camry was designed in California and built in a Toyota plant in Kentucky from mostly American parts. The car is test-driven on a track in Arizona. So, it's possible that not one piece of the Toyota your parents own was made outside the United States, even though it is a foreign car.

This same idea can be applied to so many products, from cars and trucks to television sets, furniture, and clothing.

Globalization has helped to improve living conditions in lesser-developed countries. Many people who didn't have access to basic necessities now have better food choices, basic shelter, and decent clothing, and live longer and healthier lives because of globalization. Some of the world's fastest economic growth and development are occurring in some of the poorest countries, such as India, China, and Indonesia.

The Anti-Globalization Argument

The term "anti-globalization" is used to describe the opinion of people and groups that oppose globalization. Some countries may adopt anti-globalization stances, making it harder for people, goods, and culture to spread to and from those countries. Those who are anti-globalization believe that globalization can have a negative impact on employment, culture, and the environment.

Globalization has given companies the opportunity to establish themselves in other nations. Some companies have used this as a way to save money and pay workers in developing countries less than they would pay workers in the developed countries where they are based. Some countries do not have strong health, labor, and safety laws, which are in place to protect workers from harmful chemicals, limit the number of hours a company can require of workers, and guard workers from workplace hazards. Many companies have moved their manufacturing operations to countries where these laws do not exist.

Without these protections, companies are able to make their employees work long hours for unfair pay and put their health at risk by making them work in unsafe conditions. The abundance of cheap labor in poorer, developing nations is

Globalization can create jobs in nations where employment is badly needed. Here, more than 2,500 Haitians work in a factory creating Levi's jeans and Hanes brand clothing.

giving rich, developed ones no reason to solve the problem of economic inequality between nations. While these workers are free to leave their jobs, they may not have another job to go to. That means they will not have an income and will not have a

way to make money to support themselves or their families.

Another result of jobs being sent overseas is increased competition between workers. Millions of American workers are now facing more competition from workers in less developed countries who are willing to work for far lower wages. In 2004, the AFL-CIO (a leading labor union) reported that an estimated 406,000 U.S. jobs were sent overseas, compared to 204,000 jobs in 2001.

A loss of cultural identity can occur when two or more cultures collide. There is a risk that each country could lose some of the aspects of its heritage that make it unique. There is also a risk for Westernization, which is the process in which non-Western societies adopt Western culture. "Western culture" refers to the cultures of European countries and the United States. It is a combination of industry, technology, law, politics, economics, lifestyle, diet, language, religion, and values. Some underdeveloped countries may become more modern or less traditional due to the influence of Western ideals, resulting in dramatic changes to their age-old culture.

While globalization can help inspire the solving of our environmental problems, it can also add to these problems. In the same way that health, labor, and safety laws can differ from country to country, so, too, can environmental regulations. For example, some countries allow businesses to be less concerned with the pollution generated from manufacturing and do not limit the amount of pollution that a company generates, causing widespread environmental dangers.

The Impact of Globalization

The positives of globalization often seem to outweigh the negatives. It can increase the wealth of poorer countries. It creates employment. It can result in global problem solving through shared approaches to pressing issues like protecting the environment or curing deadly diseases. It brings nations together to help one another in times of crisis. Globalization has the potential to make our world a better, more cooperative and peaceful place to live in.

Ten Great Questions
to Ask a Financial Adviser

1. Should I invest in foreign companies?

2. Are there risks to investing in companies that have a global presence?

3. Can any financial adviser manage stocks and investments in global companies?

4. What are offshore investments?

5. What is diversification?

6. What happens to my overseas investments if there is a war or other international crisis?

7. Is there an international regulatory agency monitoring and overseeing global markets like the SEC does for the U.S. economy?

8. Does my financial adviser need additional certifications or licenses to give me advice?

9. Do I pay American taxes on my foreign investments? Would I pay foreign taxes on them?

10. How are foreign investments different from U.S.-based investments?

CHAPTER THREE

The Effects of Globalization

Globalization can be exciting to watch. Its effects can be felt in all areas of people's lives. It can lead to an increase in the variety of products you buy, the kinds of foods you eat, the languages you speak, the kinds of cars you drive, and the places you travel to or work in.

Think about all the items you own, from your clothes and toys to your books, movies, board games, and video games. Many of these products were created, designed, manufactured, or developed in foreign countries. Globalization has opened up a worldwide market for companies. Today, people have access to many products from different countries. When you go shopping, you now have access to a lot more goods.

Globalization's effects reach farther than consumption, however, to include working together as a global community to solve a range of problems, from diseases and illnesses to environmental concerns. As we've seen so far, globalization has in many ways drawn the world closer. As a global community, we share responsibility for the effects globalization has on the world.

On the Environment

Globalization has drawn attention to the environment, which affects all of us. Global warming and other environmental concerns, such as melting glaciers and ice caps, air pollution, dwindling supplies of freshwater, and the dramatic changes in our climate, affect every human being on the planet. Because of this, there has been an increase in the number of worldwide environmental organizations that are working together to help coordinate international environmental policies.

The mission of the United Nations Environment Programme (http://www.unep.org) is to provide global leadership and encourage international partnerships that promote the health of the environment worldwide.

The United Nations Environment Programme helps developing countries put into practice environmentally sound policies. It was created in June 1972, following the United Nations Conference on the Human Environment. The

Greenpeace activists hold up a banner in front of an American Seafoods fishing vessel in the Bering Sea off the coast of Alaska. The activists believe that the ship is overfishing in the area and destroying the North Pacific ecosystem.

organization is headquartered in Nairobi, Kenya, and has six regional offices covering the geographic areas of Africa, Asia and the Pacific, Europe, Latin America and the Caribbean, North America, and western Asia. According to its Web site, the United Nations Environment Programme's mission is to "provide leadership and encourage partnership in caring for the environment by inspiring, informing, and enabling nations and peoples to improve their quality of life without compromising that of future generations."

Greenpeace is one of the world's most effective and attention-getting environmental activist groups. It is dedicated to the protection and conservation of the environment and the promotion of peace throughout the world. The organization has worked hard to make a number of positive environmental changes around the globe. It was successful in persuading major computer and electronics makers like Dell, Hewlett-Packard, Apple, and Sony Ericsson to eliminate the use of toxic chemicals in the manufacture of their products. Greenpeace also takes on land developers that are more interested in making money by building in natural areas than in protecting delicate and endangered ecosystems. For example,

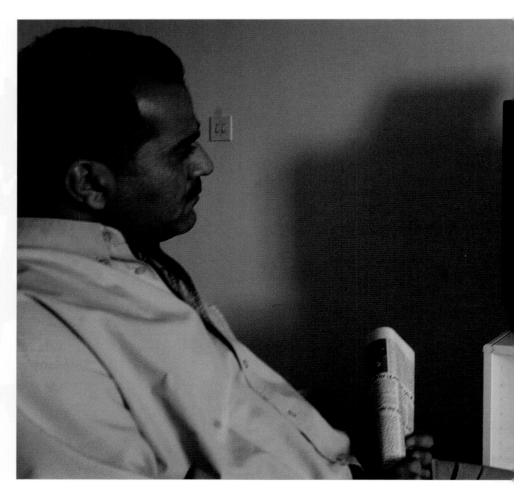

An Iraqi man watches breaking news on an international cable news network. Globalization has made it possible for people around the world to be connected and share information and experiences despite geographic distances or cultural differences.

it secured a rare victory in preserving a large area of the Amazon rain forest from being destroyed by loggers. Greenpeace has a worldwide presence, with national and regional offices in more than forty countries.

On Communication

Communication is an important element of globalization. Thanks to globalization, there has been an increase in information flowing between countries. People around the world are more connected to each other than ever before. Both the Internet and satellite television have made it possible to read newspapers, watch news broadcasts, and see movies and shows originating in foreign countries. As societies and economies embrace new communication technologies, the peoples of the world become a closer-knit community, despite the great physical and cultural distances between us.

Let's look back at a historical event that shows how news can impact the world and connect us all. The day is

September 11, 2001. You live and work in New York City, but today you are in Paris, France, on a business trip. It is early afternoon, Paris time, and you take a break from your meetings to go back to your hotel room. You turn on the television and flip through the channels. Suddenly, on one of the twenty-four-hour cable news stations, you see an image of the Twin Towers of the World Trade Center in New York City on fire. You sit and watch history unfold, live and unedited on the television set. You might be alone in your hotel room in Paris, but at the same time you are connected to millions of others who are watching the very same images at the very same moment from locations all around the world. You are all sharing the same experience at the same time.

Now, imagine what it must have been like on December 7, 1941, when Japanese forces attacked Pearl Harbor in Hawaii. The Internet did not exist in the 1940s, and neither did CNN. Television, for that matter, was in its infancy, with commercial television stations just beginning to get broadcasting licenses from the government. It took hours for news of the surprise attack to reach most Americans, mostly through their radios. It took more than an entire day before the full story, along with photographs of burning and sinking battleships, made it into newspaper articles and television news reports. Gradually, word spread farther and farther until the whole world knew of the tragedy, several days after the attack on Pearl Harbor.

Globalization has made it possible for magazines, newspapers, and other news outlets to share information on global events quickly and accurately. CNN, founded in 1980, is one of the world's leading news agencies. It has international divisions that deliver the news in Spanish, Turkish, Korean, and Japanese.

Major news publications, such as *Time* magazine, have international editions. *Time*, first published in the United States, now has a European edition called *Time Europe*, which is published in London, England. *Time Europe* covers Europe, the Middle East, Africa, and Latin America. An Asian edition, *Time Asia*, is based in Hong Kong. The South Pacific edition, covering Australia, New Zealand, and the Pacific Islands, is based in Sydney, Australia. Both global reporting and international offices increase our understanding of those who live in different parts of the world.

On Culture

Globalization can expose people to new ideas and experiences. These ideas are often adopted, and the values and traditions of a culture can change and evolve. As a result, if the change is extreme or sudden enough, it may result in a loss of cultural identity.

Food is an area in which this occurs most commonly. In many countries, food is an integral part of culture. But with globalization,

At a Starbucks cafe in the Middle Eastern nation of Qatar, two men talk over a cup of coffee.

outside influences can change the role that food plays in a culture. Take, for example, Starbucks, the American coffee company. Originally, Starbucks was a company that sold coffee beans. It did not sell brewed coffee in its stores. This all changed when Howard Schultz, the company's chief executive officer (CEO), traveled to Italy and observed the importance of coffee to the Italians.

Coffee in Italy is more than a drink. It is part of the Italian way of life. Italians sit in cafes and leisurely savor a cup of coffee. In the United States, however, it is common for people to buy a cup of coffee and take it with them to the office or to drink in the car while driving to work. Schultz saw an opportunity to change the way that Americans drink coffee. He made Starbucks cafes places to sit, relax, and sample different brews of coffee while casually meeting with friends or working on a laptop.

On Energy

Globalization has led to an increase in energy use worldwide. There are many different types of energy. There are fossil fuels, which are formed in the earth from plant or animal remains. Oil is one of the most popular fossil fuels. Nuclear power is energy that is generated through nuclear fission, which occurs when one atom splits into two. There are also renewable and alternative energy sources. These sources include biofuels, ethanol, wind power, hydrogen power and fuel cells, solar power, and hydropower. Renewable energy is using existing flows of energy, as well as natural processes, to generate energy for use. Supplies cannot be depleted or used up. Instead, they renew or replenish themselves or are constantly available.

A Chinese man cycles past the chimneys of a coal-burning power plant in Shenyang, in northern China. Globalization has increased fossil fuel–based energy usage throughout the world. As a result, world leaders are beginning to take a more active role in fighting global warming.

Water is a great example of a renewable energy source. Hydropower plants can create energy from the flow of water. The amount of available energy in moving water is determined by how fast or slow it flows through a riverbed or over a waterfall. The water flows through pipes called penstocks. As it flows through penstocks, it turns large turbines, which cause generators to produce electricity. This electricity is carried to users by power lines.

There is more energy usage today worldwide than ever before. Since 1980, the amount has increased by 57 percent globally. The United States has seen an increase of 28 percent. This amount of energy usage is equivalent to having twenty-two lightbulbs burning nonstop for every person on the planet.

Two countries whose energy usage has increased the most are India and China. Both countries are quickly developing more businesses and building more manufacturing plants. India and China also have huge populations. The more people that live in a country, the more energy that country uses.

Globalization has allowed these now developing countries to make great advances in terms of technology and prosperity. With these advances come more energy-consuming tools, machines, cars, and appliances, just like those the Western world has enjoyed for decades. The result, however positive to these nations' citizens, is an enormous and growing strain on the earth's resources and ecological health.

On Health

Globalization is promoting the rapid spread and effective treatment of highly contagious diseases. It isn't difficult to imagine how increases in international commerce and the movement of

Globalization can result in the rapid spread of contagious diseases. In Massachusetts, a Dragon Mosquito Control employee sprays a swamp area to control the mosquito population, which can carry the recently arrived West Nile virus, among other native and exotic illnesses.

people might influence health. More products are made and sold in more places around the world than ever before. People now travel farther and to more exotic locations, placing them in contact with other people in areas where specific diseases are found.

This greater movement of goods and people increases the chance for the spread of certain diseases around the world. Just like products, diseases can travel across oceans and national borders. So, diseases like AIDS, malaria, and tuberculosis can infect more people. Mosquitoes that carry malaria have been found aboard planes thousands of miles from their primary habitats. The outbreak of mad cow disease in several European countries is another example of how trade can promote the spread of dangerous diseases.

Mad cow disease was first discovered in 1986 in cattle raised in Great Britain. The disease is an incurable, fatal brain disease that affects the nervous system of a cow. It causes the animal to act strangely and lose control of its ability to do normal things, such as walk. It is believed that people who ingest poorly cooked beef from an infected cow can contract the deadly human version of this disease.

In 2007 and 2008, tainted Chinese milk products and pet food created a worldwide health scare. These are examples of how trade can promote the spread of dangerous diseases and negatively affect the safety of the food supply.

Globalization can provide the solution as well as the problem, however. It can improve access to medicines, medical information, and training that can help treat or cure diseases. Drug companies and governments now have the ability to ship drugs to remote parts of the world affected by epidemics, providing medical care to areas that they might not have been able to reach before.

On the Development of Poor Countries

Through globalization, poorer countries can raise their standards of living by trading and partnering with rich countries in order to create economic growth. The money made through trading and inviting foreign companies in to set up shop allows governments to provide better health care, education, and safety to their people. This is called development.

According to the World Bank, which is a vital source of financial and technical assistance to developing countries,

The "McDonaldization" of the World

American companies can have a strong influence on the customs of other countries. McDonald's is one company that has had a profound effect on children's behavior in China. In the past, it was not considered proper for Chinese children to buy food with their own money. Instead, they were expected to eat the food that their parents chose for them. With its fun-loving clown mascot and kid-friendly Happy Meals, McDonald's markets heavily to children. Because of this, Chinese children began to show an interest in choosing their own food when going to McDonald's. After some time, it became a more common practice for Chinese children to select and buy food with their own money.

McDonald's also popularized birthday parties in China. Festivities marking a child's birth date were not often held in China. McDonald's helped influence this new tradition by successfully promoting American-style birthday parties as part of its marketing strategy. This shows that the spread of American companies in foreign countries can have unexpected cultural consequences.

poverty worldwide has decreased due to globalization. In 2005, about 1.4 billion people in the developing world were living on less than $1.25 a day, compared to 1.9 billion people in 1981.

Globalization is creating opportunities for poor countries to partner with rich countries, giving poor countries greater access to wealth over time. When a company builds a manufacturing plant in a developing country, that country's citizens have access to jobs. Sometimes, these jobs come with training so that workers know how to use the necessary equipment. This is a form of education. The money the workers take home with them allows them to buy better food, clothes, and housing for their families. Perhaps they can even save for a formal education for their kids, who will then go on to more comfortable lives with more opportunities than their parents had.

As the economy in these poor countries grows, the nations, their citizens, and their infrastructure (roads, bridges, tunnels, railways, airports, sewers, wells, etc.) become more developed. Globalization has had a big and positive impact on many of these nations.

CHAPTER FOUR
The Best the World Has to Offer

One of the best things about globalization is that it allows people to experience different cultures. Just because someone was born in France does not mean that he or she is limited to speaking French, eating French food, reading French books, and watching French films. A French person—or an American, or an Italian, or a Chinese person—can vacation in places around the world. He can eat sushi, pizza, or lo mein noodles. He can listen to bhangra or rap. He can play baseball or practice yoga. He can read books and magazines in any number of languages. Globalization allows us to explore and experience other cultures, making our lives richer and more exciting.

Americanization of the World, or a Free Exchange of Cultural Influences?

As globalization spreads and many American companies expand into foreign countries, the idea of Americanization has emerged as a concern. "Americanization" is a term that describes the dominating and transformative influence the United States has on the cultures of other countries. American television, film, and music are considered to be the biggest agents of Americanization

Matt Groening, the creator of *The Simpsons*, a popular American cartoon, poses with his fictional television family. *The Simpsons* is among the most watched television shows internationally.

in other countries. American TV shows are broadcast around the world. According to a recent survey by *Radio Times*, the American cartoon series *The Simpsons* and the dramas *Lost* and *Desperate Housewives* are among the most watched shows internationally.

The most popular television show around the world is *CSI: Crime Scene Investigation*.

Yet, just as Americanization influences other countries, other countries influence the culture of the United States. This is not a new phenomenon. The United States has long absorbed influences from around the world, beginning with those of its former colonial masters: France, Spain, the Netherlands, and Great Britain. Its long history of immigration has expanded the range of influences dramatically. Indeed, the United States is a nation of immigrants. It is defined by the immigrant experience. As such, it provides a great example of how cultures come into contact and communicate with each other, trade influences, and ultimately create something original and powerful—a new culture with its own evolving traditions.

Just like food and television shows, sports have gone international. These days, among the most popular physical activities for North American children are Asian martial arts like judo, karate, and tae kwon do.

Many American products are not as all-American as they may seem. Levi Strauss, the creator of blue jeans, was a German immigrant who came to America and settled in San Francisco, California. He created jeans by combining denim

cloth, which was originally woven in a French town, with genes, a style of pants worn by sailors from Genoa, Italy. So, Levi's jeans are, in fact, an American twist on French fabric and Italian style. There are many similar examples of distinct cultures spreading, mixing, and becoming popular in different parts of the world, far from their origins.

Sports often spread across the globe and become fixtures in their new homelands. Many of the world's most popular sports, most notably soccer, came by way of Britain or Latin America. Both football and baseball have at least some of their origins in England. Asian martial arts like judo, karate, and kickboxing are now widely practiced by people of all ages worldwide. Yoga, which originated in India, has also swept the world.

Food is another area in which tastes have changed. In the United States, there are hundreds of fast-food restaurant chains like McDonald's, Burger King, and Wendy's. But in England, the favorite takeout food is Indian. In fact, Indian restaurants outnumber McDonald's six to one in England. And despite the hamburger's central importance to Americans, pizza is actually far more popular worldwide.

Fashion is another influential cultural force that has spread from country to country. Some of the biggest fashion houses and

Chinese teenagers sit in front of a large Coca-Cola billboard in Beijing, China. Coca-Cola products can be found in countries around the world.

designers in the world are from Europe. Gucci, Armani, and Versace are all Italian designers. Chanel and Hermès are French. Sweden's Hennes & Mauritz (known as H&M in America) and Spain's Zara compete against the American stores Gap

and Old Navy. American sneaker companies like Nike and New Balance compete against international companies, such as Adidas (Germany), Reebok (Great Britain), and Fila (Italy).

American exports are often tailored to local tastes. MTV Asia promotes pop stars from Thailand and plays rock music sung in Mandarin, a Chinese dialect. MTV Europe features European singers and bands, and it even hosts a European version of the MTV Video Music Awards. CNN en Español offers a Latin American view on world news.

The Coke Side of Worldwide Life

The Coca-Cola Company is the world's largest beverage company and one of the biggest corporations in the United States. It is best known for

53

Coca-Cola, a soft drink invented by John Stith Pemberton in 1886. The company now makes more than four hundred different beverages. These include Diet Coke, Cherry Coke, Vanilla Coke, Sprite, Minute Maid juices, and Powerade sports drinks. The company's biggest seller, however, has always remained Coca-Cola.

The company has a huge global presence. Coca-Cola operates in more than two hundred nations and has more than three hundred bottling partners worldwide. Every two days, one billion Coca-Colas are sold. The company spends $1 billion annually on advertising and marketing worldwide to make sure that its products remain highly visible and attractive.

In all countries where it is bottled, Coca-Cola helps grow the local economy. Coca-Cola does this by selling its soft drink as a concentrate to bottlers, who then add water, sugar, and carbon dioxide according to a specific formula provided by the company. These bottlers are responsible for selling the product. To sell Coke, they need to buy cases, bottles, coolers, uniforms for workers, and various other items. The Coca-Cola Company encourages its bottlers to make deals with local companies to provide these materials. By doing this, Coca-Cola bottlers spend money in their own communities, spurring the local economy and generating goodwill.

How popular is Coca-Cola around the globe? Aside from being one of the most important worldwide sponsors of the Olympic Games, it is also one of the most heavily consumed beverages on the planet. According to the company's Web site, if all the Coca-Cola ever produced was contained in eight-ounce bottles and laid end to end, they would reach to the moon and back 1,677 times. Coca-Cola has been the number-one

Disney Works Its Magic

The Hong Kong Disneyland, which opened in 2005, created new jobs for local residents. The park's designers took into consideration the cultural differences in Hong Kong. They paid special attention to things that would make its Chinese visitors feel welcome. The designers were careful to include the principles of feng shui, which is the Chinese art of placing objects in harmony with their environment. They made sure to offer Chinese cuisine, and they built a garden filled with statues of Disney characters to satisfy the Chinese interest in tourist photography. To communicate with guests, the park's employees speak both English and Chinese, including the Cantonese and Mandarin dialects of China. Guide maps are printed in a number of languages in order to accommodate the park's diverse international guests.

soft drink in France since 1966. Belgium is ranked among the world's top twenty consumers of Coca-Cola products. In Italy, consumers drink an average of one hundred servings of Coca-Cola products per person each year.

McCulture: McDonald's Influence around the World

McDonald's began in 1940 when two brothers, Dick and Mac McDonald, opened a restaurant in San Bernardino,

California. The company that is now known as McDonald's, however, really took off in 1955. That is when Ray Kroc franchised the restaurant. In the McDonald's franchising system, an owner purchases the right to operate a restaurant under the

Muslim diners eat at a McDonald's in Egypt. The hamburger chain operates more than 31,000 restaurants worldwide and serves 52 million people each day.

McDonald's name and must offer standard McDonald's products and service. The owner must also follow all of the corporate rules for operating the restaurant. Kroc later purchased the McDonald brothers' restaurants and was the man who led

the growth of McDonald's from just a few scattered hamburger stands to a massive fast-food chain with a global presence.

As McDonald's expanded into international locations, the company became a symbol of globalization and the American way of life. McDonald's now operates more than 31,000 restaurants in 107 countries. It serves fifty-two million people daily. Before the introduction of McDonald's overseas, the idea of standardized fast-food restaurants elsewhere in the world was almost unknown. McDonald's became the first company to export America's love of fast food, even though not all McDonald's serve the exact same menu. In fact, McDonald's creates regional menus to conform to local tastes and customs. In Egypt, for example, you can order a

McFalafel. In Japan, a burger made of seaweed is a top seller. In Taiwan, kids' meals are served in reusable metal containers in keeping with local custom.

The company has also let popular local products influence its menus and product offerings. For instance, McDonald's in Australia was the first to serve specialty coffees. Fancy types of breads in France and Italy became sandwich rolls in those countries. In fact, if you take a look at the official Web sites of McDonald's franchises around the world, you will find that nearly all of them are locally owned. Most buy at least half their supplies from local growers. This has a positive impact on the local economy, area farmers, and prices. (The farther food travels before being consumed, the more it will cost.) McDonald's understands that buying from local farmers and producers not only cuts down on shipping costs but also creates wealth in those communities.

McDonald's has helped to change cultures, too. In the book *Golden Arches East*, by James L. Watson, McDonald's restaurants are credited with introducing the concept of forming orderly lines to wait in before ordering, as opposed to rushing the counter, as was the tradition in Korea. In Hong Kong, public bathrooms were notoriously dirty and unsanitary. McDonald's clean, sterile facilities forced competing restaurants in the city to literally clean up their acts.

It's a Small World After All: Disney Goes Global

The Walt Disney Company is a massive global corporation. It is one of the largest media, entertainment, and merchandising enterprises in the world. Brothers Walt and Roy Disney founded it in 1923. Originally, it was an animation studio, where cartoon

Disney opened its first theme parks in California (Disneyland, in 1955) and Florida (Disney World, in 1971). The Disney empire has grown to include parks in Japan, Hong Kong, and France. Here, a parade marks the fifteenth anniversary of the Disneyland Paris park, which first opened in 1992.

movies like *Cinderella*, *Snow White*, and *Fantasia* were drawn. It has now become one of the biggest Hollywood studios and the owner of eleven theme parks around the world. The company now produces videos (*Cinderella II* and *III*) and live-action films (*The Princess Diaries*), owns cable and television networks (the Disney Channel, ESPN, and ABC), and has cruise ships. It also sells toys, clothing, and other consumer products.

Based on the success of Disney World and Disneyland, the Walt Disney Company decided to explore the idea of building theme parks in countries outside of the United States. It first established theme parks in Tokyo in 1983. The Euro Disney Resort was built outside Paris, France, in 1992. Hong Kong Disney was built in 2005. When the company first decided to build these theme parks, much consideration had to be given to each country's culture and how to best respect it while introducing the population to the very American Disney phenomenon. For example, Disney representatives sampled lots of local foods to decide what to offer at the theme parks' restaurants and concession stands. They tried to steep themselves in local and national culture in order to make sure that the theme parks accurately reflected each country in a respectful and sensitive way.

When Disney was building the Euro Disney Resort in Paris, the company hired a panel of European consultants, including representatives from France, Switzerland, England, and Germany. Disney learned from this group that Europeans do not like to stand in line for their food. So, the company needed to adjust the way that it designed and operated the food courts and restaurants at the Euro Disney park. It also decided to have more restaurants and fewer snack food options because Europeans do not eat as much as Americans do. They instead linger over meals longer than most American diners. Europeans also prefer to eat outside when the weather is nice. So, when Disney was designing eating areas, it planned for more than 2,100 outdoor seats.

CHAPTER FIVE

Globalization and Immigration

The world's population has always been on the move. But, as globalization spreads to countries large and small, the world's people have become increasingly nomadic (mobile and wandering). According to the World Bank, the number of people living outside their country of origin grew during the 1990s, rising from 120 million in 1990 to about 200 million in 2008. Many are leaving their countries of origin to seek a better life and more opportunities elsewhere. Some are simply looking to improve their lot, while others leave home out of necessity. They can find no work where they live. If they hope to support their families and survive, they must leave their home countries and seek out employment elsewhere.

Just as businesses have become globalized, shifting operations to wherever the best opportunity is, so, too, have workers, who travel to where the jobs are. With the movement of people come the transfer of ideas, the introduction of new and different customs and cultures, and the threat of change to

Immigration, even during the early years of the United States' development, has always been an extension of globalization as people moved in search of employment and better opportunities.

communities around the world. While this movement has been exciting, allowing people to learn about cultures around the world, it has also created stress and resistance. The movement of people and jobs has generated dislocations, friction, and anxiety all around the world.

On the Move

Globalization has led to the increased spread, or migration, of people around the world. By increasing the flow of information, improving communication, and making transportation faster and cheaper, globalization has also increased the number of jobs available in other countries. This causes people to migrate to those countries.

The migration of people across borders is not new. People have always left their homes in search of better opportunities,

East Los Angeles is home to the oldest Latino population in the California city. Latinos are now the majority ethnic group in Los Angeles, where they contribute to the city's economic, political, and cultural might.

both within and outside of their own countries. Globalization has added a new dimension to this movement of workers, however. As businesses expand to include operations in foreign countries, globalization has made migration a necessity for

many people. Their jobs at home may get sent overseas, where people are often willing to work for less money. This leaves the people who lost their jobs unemployed and without income (money coming in). There may be no jobs in their area anymore. So, they are forced to travel to where the jobs are—in another town, county, state, or even country.

America's Immigrant Culture

More and more people who were born outside the United States are traveling to America to live and work. These people are changing America even as they adopt its ways. More than a million immigrants arrive in the United States each year, most of them from Latin America or Asia. Since 1990, the number of foreign-born U.S. residents has risen by six million to just more than twenty-five million. This is the biggest immigration wave since the turn of the twentieth century. English may be one of the world's most spoken languages, but in some parts of the United States, it is now second to Spanish. The U.S. population is expected to grow by fifty million in the next twenty-five years. Half of that increase will probably be due to immigrants and the children of immigrants.

This renewed influx of foreigners into the United States has sparked outrage and fear among some Americans. Some people fear losing their jobs to an immigrant willing to work for less. Others are not comfortable with the customs or culture of newly arrived residents. Many Americans argue that borders should be closed to all new immigration or that only people from certain countries should be allowed in the country. In some instances, immigrants have been harassed, attacked, and even killed.

What gets lost in the overheated passion of the immigration debate is the fact that all Americans (who are not Native Americans), no matter how many generations of their family have been in the country, are the descendants of immigrants. The ancestors of Americans entered the stream of globalization, most of them choosing to leave their homes for better economic, political, or personal opportunities in a new, rich, and abundant land. These early emissaries of globalization brought their cultural traditions with them and contributed to a new American culture that preached freedom, liberty, industry, and tolerance. Today's immigrants are merely adding new layers of richness to this New World culture.

Immigrants—the everyday foot soldiers of globalization who bravely forge ahead at its front lines—do not merely take the benefits and opportunities that working and living in the

MYTHS and FACTS

MYTH Globalization is new.

FACT Globalization may be moving at a much faster pace today, but it has been around for hundreds of years. For centuries, nations have bought from and sold to other countries and have established companies on foreign soil. This international exchange of goods and services is known as trade, and it is a major component of globalization.

MYTH Globalization is a force that will result in world peace.

FACT Globalization leads to the spread of culture, languages, communication, ideas, and business. But it does not mean that people around the world are always ready and willing to welcome foreign influences. The mere exchange of money, jobs, goods, and services does not necessarily eliminate long-standing suspicions or grudges between nations. Sometimes, globalization can actually increase hard feelings or resentment when people feel their native culture is under assault by a foreign one or their jobs are being lost or exported to other countries.

MYTH Globalization only helps already rich nations get even richer, making poor nations poorer.

FACT Globalization has helped developing countries expand into business areas where opportunities did not exist before. Through globalization, many nations become stronger and more economically diverse.

United States offer. For in return, they provide hard work, often in jobs that most Americans are unwilling to perform themselves. Their work and spending contribute to the local economy, even as they continue to support family members back in their home countries. They bring their cultural traditions and merge them with American culture, creating something new and stronger and richer. American culture is immigrant culture. And globalization is, and has always been, the spark of life that has created that culture and spread it across the world, allowing all to contribute to, borrow from, and share in the riches of other cultures. This is the shining promise of globalization, its most noble ideal, and its highest achievement.

GLOSSARY

bhangra A popular dance music originating chiefly in the south Asian immigrant community of England. It combines traditional Punjabi music with elements of disco and hip-hop.

biofuel A fuel composed of, or produced from, biological raw materials. Examples are wood or ethanol.

capital Another word for money or wealth, especially when used for investments and to build businesses.

consumer A person who buys or uses a product or service.

dialect A regional version of a language that is distinguished by different vocabulary, grammar, and pronunciation from other regional varieties of the same language.

ethanol A colorless liquid used as an additive to fuel.

export To send products to another country.

feng shui A Chinese practice combining spirituality and design in which a structure or site is chosen or configured so as to be in harmony with its environment, thereby promoting smooth functioning, good fortune, and positive outcomes.

fuel cell A device that continuously changes the chemical energy of a fuel (such as hydrogen) and an oxidant directly into electrical energy.

globalism A national policy of treating the whole world as a sphere for political and economic influence.

goods Products that are made and sold to consumers.

import To bring products into a country.

migration The movement of people from one country, place, or locality to another.

vegetarian Describes a dietary practice that includes the avoidance of meat and animal-derived foods and products.

Westernization The social process of becoming familiar with or converting to the customs and practices of Western civilization.

FOR MORE INFORMATION

Centre for Research on Globalisation
P.O. Box 55019
11 Notre-Dame Ouest
Montreal, QC H2Y 4A7
Canada
Web site: http://www.globalresearch.ca
The Centre for Research on Globalisation is an independent research and media group of writers, scholars,
journalists, and activists. In addition to a comprehensive
Web site, it publishes books, supports humanitarian
projects, and conducts educational outreach activities
including public conferences and lectures. The organization supports research in developing countries and
provides expert advice on the application of research
to solving problems.

International Development Research Centre
150 Kent Street
P.O. Box 8500
Ottawa, ON K1G 3H9
Canada
(613) 236-6163
Web site: http://www.idrc.ca/index_en.html

This organization helps developing countries use science and technology to find practical, long-term solutions to the social, economic, and environmental problems they face.

International Forum on Globalization
1009 General Kennedy Avenue, #2
San Francisco, CA 94129
(415) 561-7650
Web site: http://www.ifg.org
This research and educational institution is composed of leading activists, economists, scholars, and researchers who provide analyses and critiques on the cultural, social, political, and environmental impacts of economic globalization.

The Levin Institute
116 East 55th Street
New York, NY 10022
(212) 317-3500
Web site: http://www.globalization101.org
The Levin Institute focuses on key elements of globalization in its teaching, research, and public events. It prepares graduate students to learn about, work for, and manage organizations across borders and cultures.

World Trade Organization (WTO)
Centre William Rappard
Rue de Lausanne 154
CH-1211 Geneva 21
Switzerland
Web site: http://www.wto.org

The WTO is the only global international organization that
   deals with the rules of trade between nations. Its goal is
   to help producers of goods and services, exporters, and
   importers conduct their business.

The Worldwatch Institute
1776 Massachusetts Avenue NW
Washington, DC 20036-1904
(202) 452-1999
Web site: http://www.worldwatch.org
This independent research organization is recognized by
   opinion leaders around the world for its accessible, fact-
   based analysis of critical global issues.

Web Sites

Due to the changing nature of Internet links, Rosen Publishing
has developed an online list of Web sites related to the subject
of this book. This site is updated regularly. Please use this link
to access the list:

http://www.rosenlinks.com/rwe/glob

FOR FURTHER READING

Barabasi, Albert-Laszlo. *Linked: How Everything Is Connected to Everything Else and What It Means*. New York, NY: Plume, 2003.

Lechner, Frank J., and John Boli, eds. *The Globalization Reader*. Hoboken, NJ: Wiley-Blackwell, 2007.

Nelson, Sheila. *The UN and Cultural Globalization: One World, Many People*. Broomall, PA: Mason Crest Publishers, 2006.

Ritzer, George. *The McDonaldization of Society*. Thousand Oaks, CA: Pine Forge Press, 2007.

Rowntree, Lester, et al. *Globalization and Diversity: Geography of a Changing World*. Upper Saddle River, NJ: Prentice Hall, 2007.

Steger, Manfred B. *Globalization: A Very Short Introduction*. New York, NY: Oxford University Press, 2003.

Stiglitz, Joseph E. *Making Globalization Work*. New York, NY: W. W. Norton & Company, 2007.

Wolf, Martin. *Why Globalization Works*. New Haven, CT: Yale University Press, 2005.

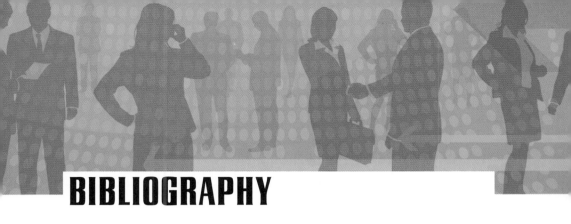

BIBLIOGRAPHY

Balko, Radley. "A Valentine to Globalization." Fox News, February 13, 2003. Retrieved October 1, 2008 (http://www.foxnews.com/story/0,2933,78416,00.html).

Bhagwati, Jagdish. *In Defense of Globalization.* New York, NY: Oxford University Press, 2007.

Buzzle.com. "Pros and Cons of Globalization." Retrieved September 18, 2008 (http://www.buzzle.com/articles/pros-and-cons-of-globalization.html).

CBS News. "Where's the Beef? Meatless McDonald's Burgers in India." April 2, 2007. Retrieved October 26, 2008 (http://www.cbsnews.com/stories/2007/04/02/asia_letter/main2640540.shtml).

Eitzen, D. Stanley, and Maxine Baca Zinn. *Globalization: The Transformation of Social Worlds.* Boston, MA: Wadsworth, 2008.

Friedman, Thomas L. *The Lexus and the Olive Tree: Understanding Globalization.* Norwell, MA: Anchor Press, 2000.

Globalist. "Coke—Globalization's Real Thing." April 4, 2001. Retrieved September 20, 2008 (http://www.theglobalist.com/DBWeb/StoryId.aspx?StoryId=2004).

Hayes, Jack. "Disney Magic Spreads Across the Atlantic; Popular U.S. Theme Park Prepares for Opening of Euro

Disney Resort Near Paris in April '92." BNET Business Network, October 28, 1991. Retrieved October 22, 2008 (http://findarticles.com/p/articles/mi_m3190/is_n42_v25/ai_11426102).

Ignatius, David. "A Global Marketplace Means Global Vulnerability." GlobalPolicy.org, June 22, 1999. Retrieved September 18, 2008 (http://www.globalpolicy.org/globaliz/special/globvuln.htm).

Knight, Deborah. "Globalization: Take Advantage of a Shrinking World." SFGate.com, August 14, 2005. Retrieved September 18, 2008 (http://www.sfgate.com/cgi-bin/article.cgi?f=/g/a/2005/08/14/padams.DTL).

LeGrain, Philippe. "Cultural Globalization Is Not Americanization." *Chronicle of Higher Education*, May 9, 2003. Retrieved September 20, 2008 (http://chronicle.com/free/v49/i35/35b00701.htm).

Longworth, Richard C. *Caught in the Middle: America's Heartland in the Age of Globalism*. New York, NY: Bloomsbury USA, 2007.

Marling, William H. *How "American" Is Globalization?* Baltimore, MD: Johns Hopkins University Press, 2006.

Overholt, William H. "Globalization's Unequal Discontents." *Washington Post*, December 21, 2006. Retrieved October 22, 2008 (http://www.washingtonpost.com/wp-dyn/content/article/2006/12/20/AR2006122001307.html).

People's Daily. "Disneyland to Bring Opportunities, Challenges to HK Tourism." February 21, 2001. Retrieved October 22, 2008 (http://english.peopledaily.com.cn/200102/21/eng20010221_62961.html).

Riggs, Fred W. "Globalization: Key Concepts." July 29, 2000. Retrieved October 22, 2008 (http://www2.hawaii. edu/~fredr/glocon.htm#CHASE1).

Stiglitz, Joseph E. *Globalization and Its Discontents*. New York, NY: W. W. Norton & Co., 2003.

White, Andrew. "From the Living Room to the World: The Globalization of Television News." Retrieved October 1, 2008 (http://homepage.newschool.edu/~chakravs/ andrew.html).

INDEX

About the Author

Laura La Bella is a full-time writer and editor who lives and works in Rochester, New York. She is the author of eight books relating to globalization, global action, and international affairs. She has profiled actress and activist Angelina Jolie in *Angelina Jolie: Goodwill Ambassador to the UN*; reported on the declining availability of the world's freshwater supply in *Not Enough to Drink: Pollution, Drought, and Tainted Water Supplies*; and examined the food industry in *Safety and the Food Supply*.

Photo Credits

Cover (top) © www.istockphoto.com/Andrey Prokhorov; cover (middle) © www.istockphoto.com/Lilli Day; cover (bottom) © Guang Niu/Getty Images; p. 1 © Mario Tama/Getty Images; pp. 6–7 © Jagadeesh/Reuters/Corbis; p. 11 © Hyundai; p. 12 © www.istockphoto.com/Brian Raisbeck; pp. 14–15 © Will & Demi McIntyre/Photo Researchers; p. 16 © Dimas Ardian/Getty Images; p. 19 © Michael Nagle/Getty Images; p. 22 © Paul J. Richards/AFP/Getty Images; p. 25 © Manan Vatsyayana/AFP/Getty Images; pp. 28–29 © Claude Richard Accidat/AFP/Getty Images; pp. 34–35, 41 © AP Photos; pp. 36–37 © Wathiq Khuzale/Getty Images; p. 39 Karim Jaafar/AFP/Getty Images; p. 43 © Darren McCollester/Getty Images; pp. 48–49 © Douglas Kirkland/Corbis; pp. 50–51 © David Katzenstein/Corbis; pp. 52–53 © STR/AFP/Getty Images; pp. 56–57 © Uriel Sinai/Getty Images; p. 59 © Francois Guillot/AFP/Getty Images; p. 63 Library of Congress Prints and Photographs Division; pp. 64–65 © Gilles Mingasson/Getty Images.

Designer: Sam Zavieh; Photo Researcher: Marty Levick